WOMAN'S EVE SYNDROME

WOMAN'S EVE SYNDROME

ELDER YOLANDA PATTERSON

Copyright © 2016 by Elder Yolanda Patterson

Glimpse of Glory Christian Book Publishing

Unless otherwise identified, all Scripture quotations in this publication are from New King James Version Study Bible. Copyright 1997, 2007 by Thomas Nelson, Inc. Some scriptures are also taken from the NIV internet version.

All rights reserved. No part of this publication may be reproduced, stored in a retrieval system or transmitted, in any form, or by any means, electronic, mechanical, recorded, photocopied, or otherwise, without the prior permission of the copyright owner, except by a reviewer who may quote brief passages in a review.

ISBN: 978-0-9833221-8-4

Printed in the United States of America

DEDICATION

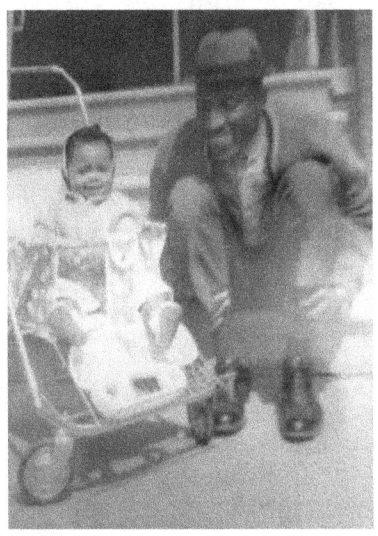

This book is dedicated to my father, the late Isaac Daniel Wilkerson, also known as I.D.

UNITY PRAYER

It is my hope and prayer that the entire body of Christ be unified in all that we do for our Lord, Jesus Christ. There is a generational curse called Woman's Eve Syndrome that has been allowed to operate in the body of Christ illegally. The devil has used it to divide the church. He is the root of division and the author of confusion. The devil will do whatever necessary to abort the plan of God. We can no longer allow the devil to cause division in the body of Christ. We must learn to work together and build up each other. God wants us to respect, support and embrace each other's spiritual positions. We are each other's keeper.

In this season, I am looking forward to serving our Savior, Jesus Christ, in Unity. Amen.

Elder Yolanda Patterson

CONTENTS

ACKNOWLEDGMENTS 9
INTRODUCTION 11
ONE: OLEAN'S GRANDDAUGHTER 19
TWO: THE LITTLE RED CHAIR 25
THREE: WHO IN HELL GOES TO CHURCH 35
FOUR: CHURCH FLOW 41
FIVE: ON BLAST PREACHER 45
SIX: WOMAN'S EVE SYNDROME 49
SEVEN: THE GREAT PHYSICIAN 59
PICTURES 67
PRAYERS 69
THE SERENITY PRAYER 93
JOURNAL 95

ACKNOWLEDGMENTS

To my Savior, Jesus Christ:
First and foremost, I must give thanks to my Savior, Jesus Christ, to my Heavenly Father, God and to my Comforter, the Holy Spirit. I thank You for giving me the inspiration, courage and knowledge to write this book.

To my husband:
Deacon John Patterson, I thank you for your love, patience and support.

To my children, stepchildren and grandchildren:
Christina, Tamika, and Victoria, I am honored to be your mother. I am thankful for my grandchildren, godchildren and spiritual daughter. Thank you all for being a special part of my life. You all are a blessing in my life. I love each of you.

To my family:
I would like to thank my brother and his wife, Mr. and Mrs. Demar Wilkerson, my aunts, uncles, nieces, nephews, sister-in-laws and brother-in-laws. You all have been such a blessing in my life. I would also like to thank my late cousin, R.L., for making me stand up for myself. You were used by God to give me the courage to write this book. I miss you dearly. I would not have much to write about

if it were not for the people God has placed in my life, to guide me along this journey.

To my friends:
The Body Family, Whitaker Family, Matthews Family, Collins Family, Armstrong Family, and Rosa, Vet, Flora, Diane, Machelle, and Elder M. Wren and wife, N. Wren, thank you all for being so kind.

To my spiritual mother and father:
I want to thank the late Pastor, Bishop Wren, for being such a great leader and mentor when you were here on earth. I know that you are rejoicing in Heaven and smiling down on me for the great work God is blessing me to carry out. I would also like to thank First Lady Annie Wren for being a blessing to me.

To my spiritual leaders of influence:
Bishop David Dumas and First Lady Gloria Dumas, I thank you both for taking me under your watch and guidance. Elder Willie D. Howard and First Lady Anetria Howard, I thank you both for allowing me to do my first trial sermon at your church. Special thanks to Pastor Andra and First Lady Shelia Wren of Lincoln Freewill Church of God and Christ, Reverend Timothy Caldwell and First Lady Sharon Caldwell of Belview Church, Pastor Kevin Lancaster and Co-Pastor Kathy Lancaster of Christian Life Center, Pastor Ben Johnson and Co-Pastor Marty Johnson of True Church, The Word Ministries with Pastor Billy Bedford and WHMA radio producer Brother Goodbread.

INTRODUCTION

LETTERS
TO MY SISTERS AND MY BROTHERS

A LETTER TO MY SISTERS

Dear Sisters,

I am writing this letter to encourage each of you on your journey as you continue to grow in love, grace, compassion, and wisdom, and carry out your purpose. We were all created by the same God, yet we are all different. We have different personalities, different perspectives, different struggles and different stories. In this season of my life, God has released me to share my story. I am not sharing my story to provoke hate, or to hurt anyone. I am simply sharing my story to provoke love. We can all use more love and spread more love. Our love cannot be lukewarm (slight, tepid, moderate). It must be extraordinary like the unconditional love of Jesus Christ. We must forgive so that we can love people unconditionally, even when they are unkind and unloving toward us.

Sisters, I know that many of you have been hurt before by family members, friends, church folks, etc. Some of you are probably at the brink of running out of compassion. I know about that all too well. I want to let each of you know that you cannot give up hope. You all must gain strength and continue being positive forces so that each of you can help another sister who may be going through something troubling in her life, maybe even something that you encountered at some point in your life. We never know what some people are dealing with, so it is important that we show how much we care—that is why God made us nurturers.

If another woman shared that she had been raped or experienced another form of abuse, we must ask ourselves if we would be willing to help her go through it or if we would ignore her cry for help. She does not need our sympathy. She needs our empathy. We have to visualize what she is going through by stepping into her shoes; that is when we can easily feel her hurt and pain.

Jesus endured so much pain and hurt for all of us. He gave His life for us. Giving His life was the greatest example of what it means to be compassionate. He cared just that much about us. He has forgiven us and cleansed us from our sins and our mistakes. He has restored us and made us queens.

It is time for us to go to a higher level and carry ourselves in a dignified manner so that we won't bring our King (God) any shame. We should always be conscious of what we do and what we say. We should not do things that will possibly make us get out of character. We should not be using profanity; it is like artificial fillers are to meat. They are usually tasteless and cheap. We can certainly not embrace or overlook being called profane names either. Since we are queens, our words should be seasoned with grace, especially if we are believers of Jesus Christ.

Yours in Christ,
Elder Yolanda Patterson

A LETTER TO MY BROTHERS

Dear Brothers,

I am writing this letter to encourage each of you on your journey as you continue to grow in love, grace, compassion, and wisdom, and carry out your purpose. I want you all to know that we share a common adversary (the devil) who has tried to cause friction between women and men, especially those who are in spiritual, leadership positions. He wants women who are in ministry to feel inferior to men who are in ministry.

Men are kings and women are queens in the site of God. He has chosen, equipped and anointed some men and women for the work of ministry. He has given us all authority. Genesis 1:26 says, "And God said, let us make man in our image, after our likeness and let them have dominion…" Genesis 1:27 clarifies who 'them' pertains to. It says, "So God created man in His own image, in the image of God created him: male and female created them."

Men, some of you find it hard to accept the fact that God has validated some women to preach the Gospel of Jesus Christ. The Bible speaks of Apostle Paul who embraced women in ministry. Early in Apostle Paul's ministry he said that he preferred women to keep silent in the church. Later in his ministry he said "There is neither Jew nor Greek, there is neither bond nor free, there is neither male nor female: for ye are all one in Christ Jesus." (Galatians 3:28).

Apostle Paul teamed up with a coupled, Priscilla and Aquila, to work together in ministry. Priscilla was a female minister. Apostle Paul lived with the couple in Corinth and they all worked together to found the church of Corinthian. Apostle Paul also lived with the couple in Ephesus for a short time. They moved there and started a church in their home. (1 Corinthians 16:9).

We too, brethren, must learn to work together in ministry. It is past time to lay aside gender issues. Women are very loyal and dedicated—many are sold out to the work of the Lord. Jesus used women throughout His entire three years of ministry on earth. A woman was at His birth (Matthew 2:1). Women ministered upon Him as He was being crucified (Matthew 27:55, Mark 15:40, Luke 23:49). A woman first saw Him at the borrowed tomb (John 20:1).

It is apparent in the Word of God that who He calls, He will also justify. Joel 2:27-29 says, "And ye shall know that I am in the midst of Israel and that I am the LORD your God, and none else: and my people shall never be ashamed. And it shall come to pass afterward, that I will pour out my spirit upon all flesh; and your sons and your daughters shall prophesy, your old men shall dream dreams, your young men shall see visions: And also upon the servants and upon the handmaids in those days will I pour out my spirit."

Jesus Christ came through 42 generations to reunite us to God and to restore our proper position in the Kingdom of God. Every sin and every curse is covered under the blood of Jesus. Men and women are once again equal. We are a perfect match for one another. Men, it pleases God when you treat women with respect. One way to show your respect is by not calling us profane names. I want to ask each of you to take this book and walk to a mirror, and then look in that mirror and imagine calling yourself a profane name. I am certain it does not feel good to call yourself a profane name. That is exactly what you are doing when you call a woman a profane name, because women are bone of your bone and flesh of your flesh. God created woman from a man's rib. Men, you all are not our enemy, and we are not your enemy. The devil is our enemy. Let's defeat him together!

Yours in Christ,
Elder Yolanda Patterson

ONE

OLEAN'S GRANDDAUGHTER

Traveling through Grosse Point with My Parents

I was born on August 12, 1964 in Detroit, Michigan. My parents migrated from the South only a few months before my birth. They bought into the dream of making automobiles. The automotive companies were paying good money to both black and white people. The opportunity to make a better life for themselves had finally come. They unfortunately found out that the North had "massas" just like the South.

They were confined to live in a predominantly black neighborhood, as if they did not have a choice to live anywhere else. My parents were supposed to be satisfied with their one acre (a two bedroom flat) and a mule (a car). It did not matter that their money was green; the color of their skin was still black. They deserved more, desired more and were determined to live a better life in the community of their choice.

My parents used to drive through Grosse Pointe, a suburban area of Detroit called Grosse Pointe. It was only a thirty minute drive from our flat. It seemed like a quick drive to a different world. We enjoyed looking at the beautiful homes. Sometimes my father drove faster than the speed limit. My mother would often remind him not to speed when we traveled through that area, because she did not want him to be stopped by the police. My father would quickly slow down after my mother reminded him. He started driving below the speed limit. My parents eventually purchased a home in that area. My father beamed with pride as he drove the speed limit in our new neighborhood.

My Father was Called a Boy

It was supposed to be an exciting, fun-filled day because we were going to visit my grandmother. While traveling through Kentucky to my grandmother's house, my father was pulled over by a policeman. I was just a little girl, but I clearly remember that incident. I noticed bright lights flashing through the back window. My heart started beating really fast. I felt scared. I loved my father more than life itself. He was a kind man. He was soft spoken and very easy going. I thought that he was going to be taken away that day, and I knew that would have been a hard pill to swallow.

My father stopped the car, and then a white police officer walked over and said, "This sure is a fancy car. Does it belong to you?" My father's voice sounded strange. It sounded like a frog was stuck in his throat. He managed to say, "Yes." The police officer replied, "Give me your license and registration, boy!" My father reached in his back pocket and gave the officer his license and registration. After the officer checked to make sure everything was valid, he gave my father back his license and registration, and then he released us.

I now understand how my father must have felt that day. And, I will never forget that day. It was a hurtful and painful day for my family. I felt like the officer was attempting to make my father feel less than a man when he addressed him as a boy. He wanted my father to know that he was not equal to officers but inferior to the color of his skin and his authority as a cop. My father did not deserve to be treated in that manner. I am certain it was not the first time he was treated as such. My father was probably called a boy and a nigger many times before the birth of his children. I am certain it hurt him, too. But the birth of my parent's children turned that hurt into sheer determination.

My Grandmother Saved My Life

My view from the back seat of my father's car as a little girl in Kentucky, then in Grosse Point, only mirrored my encounters with racism in the Deep South—this is where my grandmother lived. My grandmother's house was not far from the Alabama state line. I remember seeing colored bathrooms and white only parks. As a child, I really did not feel the effects of what was going on though. My grandmother was a civil rights activist and she did not even know it. She was loved and respected by black and white people. She was a tall glass of chocolate milk;

a beautiful, woman of husky stature. She was taller than most men. I never heard her questioned God about being a woman, nor did I hear her questioned Him about being black.

However, I did hear my grandmother talk about how big her feet were. She said that she did not know why God gave her such big feet. It was because of her big feet that my life was saved from drowning as a child. My cousins and I loved playing in the drainage ditch across from my grandparent's yard. One day as we played in the ditch we heard water rumbling like thunder. Dirty water was being released from the uptown area. I remember tumbling like clothes in a dryer. I still remember the taste of that red, mud clay. My little brother and cousins could swim, so they got out of the drainage ditch safely on their own. My cousin ran into the house to get my grandmother so that she could rescue me. Her big feet covered a lot of ground in a short length of time. She planted her feet inside the last drainage ditch, and her strong hands grabbed me and pulled me from the ditch. If she would have missed grabbing me, I would have drowned under the baseball field that was marked "For colored only."

My grandmother was a praying woman. "The effectual fervent prayers of a righteous man (and woman) availeth much." Her prayers certainly availed that day. My grandmother was also an excellent cook. She made sure her family had a good home-cooked meal every day. She always cooked more than enough. She would throw left-over scraps from the family meals out of the back door so the cats could eat them. The cats patiently waited for their meals at the back door every day. Her love for cats was no secret. I am certain they felt her nurturing spirit just as much as her family and others did.

When she took her family uptown, she refused to make an order for food or pick it up at a restaurants' back door. She was not a cat. If my grandmother could not go through the front door of a business, she kept her money in her pocket and took her business somewhere else. She was not going to settle for poor service. Her example with respect to not settling for less when she would go to certain restaurants showed me how not to ever settle for less than God's best.

I remember having a conversation with my aunt one day. She told me that my grandmother also made a vow that her children and grandchildren would never pick cotton. I am grateful that we only wore cotton and slept on cotton sheets. I will never forget the love my grandmother showed me.

WOMAN'S EVE SYNDROME   OLEAN'S GRANDDAUGHTER

TWO

THE LITTLE RED CHAIR

"A victim is always a victim at least twice—once when they are being victimized, then twice when the victim speaks up for themselves."

The Plans of the Devil will not Work

I realize that the color of my skin, my gender, my educational background, my financial status, neither my heredity nor religious beliefs makes any difference to God, or to the devil. One will always love me and the other one will always hate me. The devil hates all of us. He came to destroy our lives, but God "came that we may have life…." God created us to live an abundant and purposeful life. The devil was even created by God, but he was defeated and cast into the pit of hell a long time ago. He can no longer dwell in the presence of a Holy God. He can only visit. In 2 Corinthians 6:14, it says, "…. and what communion hath light with darkness?" That must be a miserable reality. I am certain you have heard that "misery loves company." The devil wants the same sad fate for humanity. He is determined to take all of us to hell with him. If he could, he would wipe out entire generations with just one curse.

Just think about how many ways the devil tried to kill you. Think about how many times you should have been dead, could have been dead, or would have been dead. But you are still here for a time such as now. You see, God's anointing puts a bull's-eye on our backs, and the devil knows that we are a threat to his kingdom. So that is why he works 24 hours a day, plotting to kill us. He does not care who we are or how old we are. Remember, the devil tried to kill Moses and Jesus when they were babies. He does not mind killing babies and children alike. The sooner the devil can get rid of us, the better chance he has at destroying all the lives each of us is destined to touch. He does not want to see one soul saved. He does not want any of us to grow and carry out the purpose God has planned for our lives. He will attempt to abort the mission God has purposed each of us to accomplish early on.

Everything the devil has tried to harm you and me with from birth up to this point in our lives; God has already rendered it harmless. Some of us have been lied on. Some of us have been abused and mistreated. Some of us have been rejected. Some of us have been persecuted. Some of us have even encountered some of the toughest trials and tribulations. Some of us have been troubled in our spirits. Some of us have been experiencing the enemy on every side. God tells us in Psalm 23:5, "Thou preparest a table before me in the presence of mine enemies..."

Enemies come in many forms; that includes physical abuse, mental abuse, sexual abuse, racism, sexism, rejection, betrayal, poverty and disease, just to name a few. And enemies also come from many directions, and that includes family, friends, jobs, co-workers, church folks, etc. Most enemies have one thing in common—they come from the same source, "the devil." The devil's name is the word lived if you were to spell it backward. The devil's name spelled without the letter "D" in front of it is evil.

Abuse was my Enemy

God said, "It is time to tell what happened to you as a child. It will deliver someone from feeling the same way you did." It was so hard to write this part of my book. I had to put all my trust in God who is the Author and Finisher of my faith. My sanity comes from Him. My peace comes from Him. My joy comes from Him. My wisdom comes from Him. My courage and strength come from Him, and I needed both to share what happened.

I was about four years old when it all started. I used to think that I was a mistake because I was told that so many times. I used to hear that word "mistake" over and over in my head. It took God to heal me from hearing that I was a mistake. I was told that I would never be anything. I was not told that I was pretty and smart—those compliments were not allowed. If someone said that I favored the person who I refer to as a judge, the judge would get angry. I remember a lady saw the judge and me at the store, and she said that I was beautiful. The judge immediately corrected the lady by saying, "Don't tell her that!" The lady also complimented my brother and the judge blushed. I tried so hard all my life to please the judge and, after many failed attempts, I finally realized that I had to disappear from the judge's life. That would have eased the pain. The judge was troubled by something that probably happened long ago. I just did not know what part I played.

I used to play at my little, red table during the day and I sat in the matching chair. I would pretend to have a tea party for my dolls. As the sunset, night crept into my room. My little, red chair had a different purpose at night. It turned into the judgment chair. I would be judged every night that our family did not have company. I was judged for what I did wrong. Each day I tried so hard not to mess up my room, clothes, and toys. Everything was kept in perfect line, but somehow I was still found guilty for something that I did. I would even have a panic attack if something was not in a straight line.

I would be awakened from my sleep at night, and seemingly the little, red chair waited for me in the back bedroom. Sometimes I tried to pretend that I could not wake up. That did not even matter. I still made it to the judgment chair; nothing could make it stop. The guilty verdict never stopped either. My punishment was a beaten. Every morning after, I pretended so well that not even my dolls knew what happened the night before.

A few people noticed that something strange was happening. My high school art teacher questioned me about my black eye; makeup couldn't help me hide it. I knew that I would not survive another judgment night if I said anything to them. I just had to make them think everything was perfectly fine. My extended family was not told who I really was and I did not open my mouth about that either. No one ever challenged what the judge said. If the judge said a four year old child was evil, then it had to have been true.

It appeared that there was another person living inside the judge; that person was nice to me. I was confused by that. I could not hate them both; neither could I love them both. But I had to accept them both. I had not choice. I was just a little girl who wanted to be happy. I must admit that I felt better on the days the judge took me on those fun rides to my cousins' house. I was allowed to spend the night sometimes. I slept peacefully on those nights because I did not have to be sent to the little, red chair.

The little, red chair eventually got thrown away when some of the judge's family moved in with us and slept in the back bedroom. I thought that by my little, red chair being thrown away it would erase the memories, but it didn't. I even thought that things would get better as I grew, but they didn't.

When I became a teenager, things got worse, even to the point to where I ran away from home. I wanted the judge to stop hurting me. I just wanted to be happy once and for all. I was smiling on the outside but crying out loud on the inside.

My classmates were my medicine. Only my very close friends saw glimpses of the judge. I pretended so well that I figured no one would even believe that the judge were two people.

As time progressed, I became a wife and a mother. Surely the little, scared, insecure girl was not still sitting in the little, red chair, or sitting at the little, red table. But let me tell that the Lord used that table to spread a feast before my enemy. Forgiveness, love, joy, longsuffering, and steadfastness are now on the little, red table I used for my tea parties as a little girl. I have forgiven the judge and myself for making some of the same mistakes. I am finally at peace. God turned the experience with the little, red chair into a testimony. He used the hurt and pain to build the strong woman that I am today, for His Glory.

"There is no testimony without test."

It was necessary to share my testimony about overcoming evil with the goodness of God. It is a privilege to share what God has done for me and where He has brought me from because someone else needs to hear just how good He is. He has been so good to me, even when situations and circumstances said otherwise. I have a purpose and I realize what I do for Jesus Christ will last.

The Anointing Destroys Yokes

Isaiah 10:27 says, "…And the yoke shall be destroyed because of the anointing." There is nothing that we will ever encounter in life strong enough to keep us down. God's anointing is able to rip the life out of whatever the devil tries to bind us with. Some of the trials (and they will come in multiple assaults) that you and I have faced, and even the ones that some of you may be dealing with right now, you must decree and declare that it is over. It truly will be "A-No-In-Test. Psalm 23:5 says, "…thou anointest my head with oil…" Yes, our loving, Holy Father that lives in Heaven will allow trials and tribulations to come but the oil that He anointed our heads with will destroy those trials and tribulations every time. God anoints His children's head because it controls the whole body. The anointing is "a weapon of mass destruction."

The Lord identifies His chosen vessels by anointing them before the devil and other people. David was anointed with oil poured over his head. He was a chosen vessel of God. David went through a lot of things just as some of us have gone through. Many of us have to go through some hard, hurtful, discomforting, rough, painful…trials because of the anointing that is on our lives. God did not say that He would not allow us to experience some…trials, but He did promise us that He will never leave or forsake us. So, even when we are going through…God is with us. I know for a fact that God has His angels surrounding His children every day. We are all a part of His master plan. And what He has planned for our lives will turn out for our good, regardless of what we may encounter on our journey.

The Curse is Broken

I could now pursue my own identity. The curse that tried to destroy my family was broken by the love of Jesus Christ. God gave me victory of over physical abuse, mental abuse, verbal abuse, domestic violence, poverty, divorce, racism, sexism, guillian barre syndrome, nut cracker syndrome, stroke symptoms, paralyzed lower extremities, blindness in one eye, brain tumor, severe migraine headaches, legal battles, diabetes, hypertension, bipolar disorder, rupture appendix, gall bladder removal, chronic back pain, degenerative joint disease, metal plate and titanium screw appliance to lower back, disability, gastric reflux, esophageal spasms, anatomic defect of the gastro esophageal valve, esophageal nut cracker syndrome, the eve syndrome, over 20 surgeries and medical procedures.

You may have experienced something similar as a child, and even as an adult. It may have torn you apart and caused friction in your family. It could not destroy you because you are still here. Whatever curse that may have plagued your family is broken, too. You too can experience victory today. I realize the devil is my enemy, not people. None of the curses from the devil stopped God's plan for my life. I am humbled and proud to be called a Woman.

The five conditions below have profoundly affected my life:

Bipolar Disorder is a disorder associated with episodes of mood swing ranging from depressive lows to manic highs. There are more than three million cases in the United States per year. This disorder does not have a cure but can be treated.

Guillan Barre Syndrome is a disorder in which the body's immune system attacks parts of its' own peripheral nervous system. The patient may need to be placed on a ventilator during treatment. It can be a life threatening illness. There is no cure.

Nutcracker Esophagus is a motility disorder that causes difficulty swallowing both solid and liquid foods. It can cause significant chest pain. There is no cure. It can be treated with gastric reflux diet, gerd medications, and medication that effect the muscle contraction of the esophagus. 1 out of 10,000 people have this medical condition.

Degenerative Joint and Disc Disease is a condition in which a damaged vertebral disc causes chronic pain, either low back pain in the lumber spine, or neck in the cervical spine. As the body ages, joints inflammation occurs.

Woman's Eve Syndrome is man's fear of women's influence.

THREE

WHO IN HELL GOES TO CHURCH

Sunday Morning

It was a typical Sunday morning. I planned on staying in bed the entire day. I was off the entire weekend and all I wanted to do was sleep. My body was nestled deeply inside my favorite blanket. It felt like a warm coat wrapped around me on a cold winter day. My king-sized bed made me feel like a queen. The alarm clock was singing a love song to me as usual. The thought of who would get out of bed on their day off crossed my mind, followed by the thought of maybe someone crazy or someone who is chasing their green paper (money). Since neither person described me, I just rolled right over and silenced my alarm clock and nodded off—until my conscious started hounding me.

If only my conscious would take a nap. I realized that it could not be silenced like my alarm clock. My mind, body and spirit were drained. I was sleepy and exhausted. I worked two jobs most of my nursing career. It was a grueling experience. Working the twelve hour Baylor shifts every weekend and the eight hour shifts on Monday through Friday had taken a toll on me. I felt like I just needed to rest.

Good and Evil

As I continued lying in my bed, contemplating if I was going to get up and get ready for church, I began picturing a female angel sitting on my right shoulder. Her eyes sparkled like sapphires. She was cute as a baby doll. She was wearing a pair of pink flannel pajamas. Her head was adored with a pink bonnet. The angel kept pulling up her saggy pajamas as she continually marched on my shoulder. It was obvious that she was agitated with me. "Marisa, it's time to get ready for church," the angel shouted. I said, "Oh, no she didn't just call me by my middle name." I was upset with a figure of my imagination. The angel suddenly sat down with her lips stuck out and her arms folded.

I imagined another angel appearing on my opposite shoulder. Her beauty could drop a strong man to his knees. Her red, silk gown looked as if it were spray painted on her curvaceous silhouette. The gown's split went up her legs, nearly revealing her cookie jar. It was obvious she was a high- ranking devilish diva. Her warm breath swirled in my ear as she spoke just above a whisper. She said, "Sister, from the looks of it, you need all the beauty sleep you can get. Surely missing church today won't hurt. I would not be so hard on myself if I were you. I have been known for missing church a lot lately. Who in hell goes to church?" She started laughing.

Then, all of a sudden, I heard a still small voice quote Hebrews 10:25. This power scripture says, "Not forsaking the assembly of ourselves together as the manner of some is; but exhorting one another: and so much the more, as ye see the day approaching."After hearing that scripture being echoed in my ear, I realized those angels were not my imagination. It was God giving me a perfect parable. One angel represented my spirit and the other represented my flesh. The Bible warns us in Matthew 26:41 to "Watch and pray so that we will not fall into temptation. The spirit is willing, but the flesh is weak." The battle between good and evil, right and wrong, would leave us defeated every day, if it were not for the Word of God.

His Word also tells us in Ephesians 6:12, "For we wrestle not against flesh and blood, but against principalities, against powers, against the rulers of the darkness of this world, against spiritual wickedness in high places." And it goes on to say in 1 Corinthians 10:13, "There hath no temptation taken you but such as is common to man: but God is faithful, who will not suffer you to be tempted above that ye are able, but will with temptation also make a way to escape, that ye may be able to bear it."

Satan's Permission to Attack

We must all understand that Satan has to obtain pre authorization before launching his attacks. He is allowed to use his full arsenal of weapons. He cannot operate outside of God's plans. The devil is actually being used to facilitate God's perfect will in my and your life. Satan wants to challenge God's perfect will by trying to tempt us to step outside of God's will. He also wants us to operate outside of God's timing.

God moves in seasons. Whenever we are in the wrong place at the wrong time, we miss the perfect will of God. To ensure that we don't miss our designated season, He will allow the devil's tactics to push us "toward the mark of the high calling." I really felt like I was being stretched and pushed that Sunday morning. The devil attacked my body with fatigue. He sent a demonic, sleepy spirit to detour my destiny. But, after all, it did not work as he planned.

God Gave Me Strength to Go to Church

What the devil meant for my bad, God turned it and allowed it to work in my favor as He planned. God stepped in and reminded me of what Isaiah 40:31 says, "But they that wait upon the Lord shall renew their strength. They shall mount up with wings as eagles; they shall run and not be weary, and they shall walk and not faint." I certainly needed strength that day, and God made sure I had more than enough strength. He sent my spirit an alert that I needed to be at church and that He would have a word of instruction downloaded in the morning message just for me. My mind, body and spirit got stronger and happy when I heard that. I immediately jumped out of my bed and my feet hit the floor running. The atmosphere changed. My mood even changed. With a high level of excitement, I told myself, "It's time to get ready for church."

While I was getting dressed, I could not help but think about what Isaiah 52:1 says, "Awake, awake; put on thy strength, O Zion; put on thy beautiful garments, O Jerusalem, the holy city: for henceforth there shall no more come into thee the uncircumcised and the unclean. Shake thyself from the dust; arise, and sit down, O Jerusalem: loose thyself from the bands of thy neck, O captive daughter of Zion."

I now realize that once we really accept the fact that we are in God's world and He is in control, and our Commander and Chief, the Author and Finisher of our faith, Alpha and Omega, the Beginning and the End, the God of time, the One who fights all of our battles, then the only thing we need to do is "fight the good fight of faith." We must learn to press our way despite what the devil tries to throw at us, because God has equipped us with what we need to tread over him. We must stay on our preordained specified course, and "…run with endurance the race that is set before us." (Hebrews 12:1).

WOMAN'S EVE SYNDROME   WHO IN HELL GOES TO CHURCH

FOUR

CHURCH FLOW

God's Time Zone

It is crucial that we flow in God's time zone. If we do, we will always end up in the right place at the appointed time. God's time zone moment is defined as a sudden swift brief numerical quantity of time. 1 Corinthians 15:52 is an excellent expression of God's time zone. It says, "In a Moment," in the twinkling of an eye, at the last trump: for the trumpet shall sound, and the dead shall be raised incorruptible, and we shall be changed."

God's timing operates inside of His will. You cannot have one without the other. He has pick up locations. Pick up locations are authorized spiritual levels and earthly physical locations. When He orders our steps, we will always arrive at our preordained location on time, not before or after, but right on time. His Word tells us that "The steps of a good man are ordered by the LORD: and he delighteth in his way." My preordained location for that day was my church.

Being Late is an Enemy to Your Destiny

I must admit that I was often late for church on Sunday mornings, due to being sluggish and slothful. I just wanted to lie in my bed and sleep the day away. There is no telling how many powerful moves of God I missed by being late. Each time I was late I vowed that I would prepare myself the night before. It rarely happened. I was frustrated many times. It was not a thing of beauty. It was pure chaos. I always found myself filtering through my closet to find something nice to wear. The clothes were scattered all over my bedroom. Everything I tried on was either too small or too big. It was either the wrong style or the wrong color. It seemed like I could never find a matching pair of earrings. It was a miracle to find both backs to the pair of earrings I desired to wear; one would always be missing. I could also not find my shoes or my car keys. And, my stockings were running as if they were in a marathon. I noticed that the stocking's packaging said one size fits all, but that's not true. Just like we all don't fit in the same spiritual positions.

Perhaps you may be having similar experience now. You may have found yourself being side-tracked by the devil's tactics lately on Sunday mornings. You may even be sluggish and slothful too, or it could be something else that you battle with. Either way, the devil will do whatever necessary to keep you from going to your church.

I now know that the devil's job is to interrupt our connection with God's timing. He does not want us to be where God wants us to be at an appointed time, certainly not at church because he knows that that is where we are spiritually fed, fellowship with one another, gain strength, etc. The devil will try to interrupt us by making us anxious and impatient, sluggish and slothful, confused and frustrated, and the list goes on. He will interrupt some of us by making us too early, too late, or even cause us to be absent and miss a mighty move of God.

Satan tried his best to make me miss a life-changing moment with God that Sunday morning. I have finally learned that whenever the devil throws everything, including the kitchen sink at you and me, he is aiming to block our blessing that God has already scheduled. "Whenever God starts blessings, the devil starts messing."

God's Remedy

I knew my church flow had to change and I had to change the way I was doing things. I was ready to change too. I repented for being sluggish and slothful, and told God that I wanted to be in His perfect will. He reminded me of 1 John 5:17, "All unrighteousness is sin: and there is a sin not unto death." God has been working on me over the years. "The woman I was yesterday, introduced me to the woman I am today; which makes me excited about meeting the woman I will become tomorrow."

I realize that God did not have a problem with me looking nice for church. He has no problem with me choosing to wear makeup, jewelry, or different colors and styles of clothing that is becoming of a woman. He wants us to look nice and represent Him with class. The problem was that I was spending too much time getting myself together, after I finally mustered up enough strength to get out of my bed. I wanted to do better so I prayed

to God for a remedy to combat the madness, negative energy, chaos, and evil that I seemingly faced on Sunday mornings. God answered my prayers. His remedy was for me to start committing myself to time management, organization, and preparation. They all facilitate His will. After I started doing those things, they helped me to stay within His perfect timing, and in His will. I want you to be fully assured that if God provided a remedy for me, He will certainly do the same for you, too.

FIVE

ON BLAST PREACHER

Sunday Morning Again

It was a good thing that I only lived ten minutes away from my church. I was a member of a church that was nestled away on a hillside in Lincoln, Alabama. Sunday school had just started. We divided into our imaginary classrooms. Our church was small with only one large room which was the sanctuary. The men sat on one side of the church. The women sat on the opposite side of the church. Sometimes the men sat in the choir stand for Sunday school. Just a few pews in the back of the church accommodated the small children. The hallway was the teenager's classroom. Everyone else knew to stay in their usual location.

On this particular Sunday, I experienced something that I had never experienced before. Sunday school seemed to have been fast paced. Before I knew it, we were having worship service. I was ready to hear the Word of God. My pastor preached his heart out as usual. He was a walking Bible professor of the

Word. The man was wise beyond his years. God gave him a love for His Word. The members benefited tremendously. He knew what the protocol was and the traditions of our church doctrine. He also followed Christ's instructions. I am certain he took the heat for doing that.

Put on Blast

While my pastor was preaching, he stopped and made eye contact with me. I felt like hiding under the pew. I was thinking, "What was God showing him about me?" I knew God had a blessing for me, but this was not how I had expected it to go. He continued staring at me, and then he said, "Sis. Londa, what God say you is?" Now do not get it twisted. This man was very intelligent. He knew correct grammar; that was not an issue. The issue was that he had put me on blast. I could not tell him or the congregation what God told me. I did, however, know that women were allowed to function as missionaries or evangelist. Well, at least I thought that for a long time.

So in hopes that he would move on with the message, I said, "Missionary." He did not respond. He turned and walked away, and then he looked at me and asked the same question again, "Sis. Londa, what God say you is?" I wanted to disappear. My heart started racing and my throat got dry. I immediately said, "Evangelist." He didn't say anything. He started preaching again. Shortly after, for the third time, he stopped and made eye contact with me and asked the same question again, "Sis.

Londa, what did God say you is?" I was thinking to myself the mother's board is going to faint. Those who think that I am too radical and not good enough to even be in the church are going to burst into laughter. For a brief moment, I punked out on God and my pastor! I reverted to the scared, insecure, little girl sitting in the little, red chair. I could hear the words, "You will never be anything." I finally responded, "Whatever you say, Pastor." He said, "God said you is a Preacher." I was in awe of how God used him to tell me that.

A Brand New Experience

I will always cherish what God allowed my pastor to release into my life. The preached message was rich and powerful. I was glad that I was right where God wanted me to be that Sunday. I must admit that this church was very similar to the one I used to attend in Detroit, Michigan. That was a Holiness church though. I was a teenager when I was a member there, so I did not know the difference between a Baptist church and a Holiness church. I did, however, know that there was a difference in the way one of my high school classmates in the Sunday school class carried herself. She was more graceful, confident and classy.

I wanted to know more about her because I wanted more of what she had. It would be remiss of me if I did not tell you that I was dying on the inside. I had nothing to lose. My public life was very different from how my life was behind closed doors. I thought that maybe my life could change too, so I asked her what happened to her. She simply invited me to visit her church. Up to that point, I had attended a Baptist church since I was a child. I was ready to experience something new. The very first visit I felt like I was being cleansed from things that had me bound, as the tears rolled down my face. That was one of the "best days of my life."

After the experience that day, a change was happening so fast—inside and outside of me. I was willing to do whatever necessary to love God back. I experienced that a long time ago when I lived in Detroit. I felt strongly after I visited that church that God was doing a "new thing" in my life. I realized different church denominations don't matter. I have finally realized that God made me on purpose, and I am glad about where He is taking me.

SIX

WOMAN'S EVE SYNDROME

Women are Powerful

I am a female citizen of the United States of America. My rights should not be different from a male citizen of the United States of America. I have the right to enlist in the armed forces. I can give my life to serve and protect my country. On June 4, 1919, my right to vote was made law in the US Constitution's 19th Amendment. I can exercise my right to vote for a female that is running for the highest position in the United States, the President. Fortune 500 companies have female CEOs. Some women own their own businesses. Women are the most educated people in the United States. We pump billions of dollars into the economy each year.

The Syndrome that Divides Women and Men

Why is that women are often treated like second class citizens? Why are women still not welcomed to preach in some churches that sit on the soil of this great nation? I questioned God about this and He answered me through a divine revelation. God said this to me, "Men are still operating under a generational curse called Woman's Eve Syndrome." God defined Woman's Eve Syndrome as man's fear of woman's influence.

God said that men still blame women for the fall from grace in the Garden of Eden. Men trust issues with women began in the book of Genesis in the Bible. The word Genesis means the beginning. A Gene is fundamental, physical and functional unit of heredity. Woman's Eve Syndrome was the first curse that infected a man's DNA. This curse would be carried through the male's bloodline from one generation to another.

A syndrome is defined as a collective set of symptoms that indicates a malfunction or infection in one or more of the body's systems. If the cause of the infection is not identified and treated, death will occur. Woman's Eve Syndrome is very similar to a natural syndrome. The cause must be identified and treated or a spiritual death will occur.

The origin of Woman's Eve Syndrome began in Genesis 1:26. It says, "And God said, let us make man in our image, after our likeness and let them have dominion over the fish of the sea, and over every creeping thing that creepth upon the earth." If you noticed, God said, "And let them have dominion over the fish..." God already had a preordained time to create a woman. It says in Genesis 2:7, "And the Lord, God formed man of the dust of the ground, and breathed into his nostrils the breath of life; and man became a living soul." God told man to dress and keep the Garden of Eden. He also instructed man not to eat from the tree of the knowledge of good and evil. God told man in Genesis 2:17 that if he ate from that tree, he would surely die. He began to call man Adam after he formed a fatherly relationship with his first human creation. It goes on to say in Proverbs 2:1-6, "My son, if thou wilt receive my words, and hide my commandments with thee; so that thou incline thine ear unto wisdom, and apply thine heart to understanding…Then shalt thou understand the fear of the LORD, and find the knowledge of God. For the Lord giveth wisdom: out of his mouth cometh knowledge and understanding."

God decided that it was the perfect time to create woman. Genesis 2:18 says, "And the Lord God said, it is not good that the man should be alone; I will make him a help meet for him." God defines a help meet as an equal partner that assists. He also says a help meet is a perfect match. In the natural when a person is in need of blood or an organ, they must find the perfect donor or the body will reject the transplant or blood transfusion. God wanted a perfect match for Adam so he took a rib from his side. Adam could not reject his own flesh. God made a perfect match for man when he created woman. Genesis 2:23 says, "And Adam said, this is now bone of my bones, and flesh of my flesh: she shall be called Woman, because she was taken out of Man."

Adam was the first man to set the bar very high. His choice

of calling the first female a woman was epic. He acknowledged the fact that his mate's womb would bare mankind. The respect and admiration for woman by Adam was obvious in Genesis 2:23. Unfortunately it did not last long. In Genesis Chapter 3, it shows where woman betrayed the trust of God, and her husband. She listened to the serpent. He told her that God does not want her as smart as he was. Woman was not created when God gave man instructions not to eat from the tree of knowledge. Woman only knew what her husband told her.

Most women will probably admit that if we find out that our mate did not tell us the whole truth, we will eventually find out the part that was not told to us. The Bible does not tell us exactly what Adam told her, but it does tell us exactly what God told Adam. Woman only knew that she should not eat from that tree. Woman may have felt like she got shafted by God and her husband. The serpent did not attack woman because she was the weaker vessel. None of that existed. Adam and woman were equal. They were a perfect match.

The Curse of the Syndrome

The serpent tempted woman because he wanted her womb to birth the curse of Woman's Eve Syndrome. In Genesis 3:12, it says, "And the man said, the woman whom thou gavest to be with me, she gave me of the tree, and I did eat." God had to punish everyone involved with the fall from grace in the Garden of Eden. Through one man's transgression, sin entered into the world. The Bible says that the wages of sin is death. Disobedience carries a very hefty price tag. The serpent's punishment was to crawl on his belly all the days of its life.

God placed enmity between the serpent and woman and enmity between their seed. At that time, a woman's punishment was increase pained and sorrows during childbirth. A woman was no longer a man's equal. He would now rule over her. A man's punishment came in Genesis 3:17, "And unto Adam he said, because thou hast hearkened unto the voice of thy wife, and hast eaten of the tree, of which I commanded thee, saying, Thou shalt not eat of it: cursed is the ground for thy sake; in sorrow shalt thou eat of it all the days of thy life."

Woman's Eve Syndrome name came in Genesis 3:20, "And Adam called his wife's name Eve; because she was the mother of all living." Adam no longer had the same respect, trust and admiration for God's female creation. He no longer called her woman (the womb that would bare mankind). Adam called her Eve after he got his punishment from God. Adam blamed Eve for having to work by the sweat of his brow. He also knew he had to die because of the influence of Eve.

My Experience with the Syndrome

Do you remember me telling you about how my father was treated when he was stopped by the policeman in Kentucky? Well, the way my father was treated reminds me of how I was treated when I started preaching the Gospel of Jesus Christ. God is the One who called, chose, validated, qualified and ordained me...Some people do not believe in women preachers, but God can use both women and men to preach. I was first a minister and then He elevated me to the spiritual office of an elder.

Just like that police officer made my father feel like he was not equal to him by addressing him as a boy; I am not called an elder by other clergy who wants me to feel that I am not their equal because I am a woman. They also feel the need to keep me in my so-called place. What I mean by this is that some people do not want you to fully operate in the office in which God has appointed you to, so they will do and say things to belittle you. If you are in ministry, wouldn't you find it strange if someone addressed you with a different title than the one Your Heavenly Father gave you? I graciously tell people what the title is that God gave me, which is Elder Yolanda Patterson. Some people still address me with other titles: missionary, sister or evangelist, just to name a few. To add insult to injury, my spiritual title has even been changed on church programs.

There have been times that I have been frowned upon while standing beside other elders who were men when they were called to pray at the altar. I have also been told not to sit in the pulpit at some churches. I felt like I was being segregated simply because I am a woman. It seems as though the pulpits in those churches were only for male clergy. A mindset that is conditioned to only accept men in the pulpit promotes segregation. Think about it. How is the experience that I had any different than what my parents dealt with when they were not allowed to live in a community where they wanted to because the color of their skin? That was segregation, too.

I was not going to let those experiences that I faced in those churches tear me apart. However, I allowed them to help shape and make me. I now realize that God would never allow anyone to separate me (or any other woman in ministry) from my divine destination. Romans 8:38-39 says, For I am persuaded that neither death, nor life, nor angels, nor principalities, nor powers, nor things present, nor things to come, nor height, nor depth, nor any other creature, shall be able to separate us from the love of God, which is in Christ Jesus, our Lord." Love always conquers hate. Those who are forgiving like me are often those who love real hard. Loving those who mistreated me and hurt me is what I will continue doing because I know what our Heavenly Father encourages us to do in Luke 6:27, "...Love your enemies, do good to them which hate you."

The Power of a Virgin Woman

God already had a plan to redeem us, His children, in due season. God knew that sin would enter into this world through Eve's womb. God entrusted a virgin woman named Mary to carry the fate of the whole world inside her womb. This same woman would be used to bring Jesus out of the closet. The first public miracle by Jesus was done at the request of a woman. He responded to her request by turning the water into wine. Jesus also publicly restored respect and admiration to womankind. In John 2:-4, it says, "Jesus saith unto her, woman, what have I to do with thee? Mine hour is not yet come."

The first person to preach the good news that Christ had risen from the dead was a woman named Mary Magdalene. She was a prostitute whose honor was restored through giving her life to Jesus. She will always be remembered for washing the feet of Jesus with her hair.

The Bible says in Galatians 3:13, "Christ hath redeemed us from the curse of the law, being made a curse for us: for it is written, cursed is every one that hangeth on a tree." The curse is everyone who hangs on a tree. The cross was the tree that Jesus hung on and died for all humanity. The wages of all sin has been paid in full. He became a curse so that we could be free from any curse.

A quick review of this divine revelation

Woman's Eve Syndrome is man's fear of woman's influence. It has caused spiritual stagnation, hurt and pain, chaos; division in the church…This syndrome is a generation curse that was birth through the first female creation of God. The first woman, Eve, disobeyed God when she ate from the tree of knowledge of good and evil. The first woman also gave her husband the first male creation of God, the forbidden fruit to eat. Adam, the first male creation, succumbed to the influence of his wife and ate the forbidden fruit. The first woman's womb conceived the serpent's seed of sin. The first man gave permission for the serpent's seed to impregnate his wife by eating the forbidden fruit. Sin was thereby birthed into the world through the first woman's womb. This caused the spiritual and physical death of mankind.

Romans 5:12 says, "Wherefore, as by one man sin entered into the world, and death by sin; and so death passed upon all men, for that all have sinned." The scripture said by one man. If the first man, Adam, did not give his consent by eating the forbidden fruit, the seed of the serpent would have been aborted. Just imagine if a man was married to a woman and she cheated on him and became pregnant by another man. A death will occur, physically and spiritually. The marriage would probably end in divorce. The man would not trust the woman anymore. There will be anger and hostility between the two of them. It would be a crushing blow to a man's ego and state of mind. The man would find it embarrassing that the woman has his last name. The man would blame his cheating wife for destroying their happy home. The relationship between that man and woman would never be the same. God knew that He had to restore the spiritual and physical relationship between man and woman, in order to redeem man's seed.

Let us Pray

Dear Heavenly Father, please hear our prayer in the name of Your Son, Jesus Christ. Thank You, Father, for destroying the works of the devil. Thank You for Your forgiveness and restoration. There is nothing that can ever separate us from You again. Thank You for giving us the power over Woman's Eve's Syndrome. We send this curse back to the pit of hell, in Jesus' name. There is no more guilt. There is no more shame. We are free from every sin and curse, because who the Lord sets free is free indeed. All enmity between God and His creation is long gone. We all can walk together with God once again in "the cool of the day." Amen.

SEVEN

THE GREAT PHYSICIAN

Be Made Whole in Your Body

Hosea 6:1 declares, "Come, and let us return unto the LORD: for he hath torn, and he will heal us; he hath smitten, and he will bind us up." When we become sick in our bodies, there will be signs and symptoms of a disease process operating inside of us. We normally seek out a physician to diagnose the problem and treat our illness with medication. "A physician is a person qualified to practice medicine, one who is a healer."

Depending on the urgency of our condition, we will rush to the emergency room to be seen by a doctor. If our condition is not so bad, we will call our primary physician to schedule an appointment. When we call their office, we must know their name, right? That's just how we should be about our Heavenly Father. We should not only call Him "The Great Physician," we should also know Him as our personal "Great Physician," the One who heals us from all of our infirmities, physically and spiritually. We must also have confidence in knowing that He will release His healing power through doctors when we are physically sick.

So after we make an appointment with our primary physician, we will go to their office on the scheduled date given to be seen and receive proper care for our condition. The physician usually has a generic questionnaire form that asks personal and sensitive information. For example, "Is there a deviation of normal functioning within the body? Is there objective evidence of disease such as abnormal bleeding? Is there any subjective evidence of disease such as pain and weakness? How long have you noticed a change? How long has this been happening? What makes it worse or better? Have you been self-medicating? What meds and treatments are you currently using? Have they been non-effective and/or have you discontinued them? Are you open-minded or close-minded to trying a different treatment? Are you willing to be a proactive member of your plan of care? Are you fully invested and committed to finding a cure?

The physician will review all previous medical history. He or she will usually order blood work and any other necessary tests. The physician will start the process of elimination as the data is collected. Based on preliminary data, the physician may find it necessary to begin immediate treatment and medication. Some may see that as putting a band aid on it until bleeding has stopped, and then find out with additional investigating why the bleeding occurred. The patient and the physician must have an open and honest relationship, and the line of communication is extremely vital to ensuring the best outcome. The patient must have access to the physician and vice versa. Moving quickly is also vital as the patient's life may be in grave danger. This is called holistic care; the whole body of the patient is under treatment. Timing is of essence and must be held in high regards. The patient's body systems may be malfunctioning in an aggressive manner. Reviewing the entire pool of information will be crucial in a speedy, complete recovery.

Providing this insight may remind you of God's timing and His perfect will that was discussed in a previous chapter. We must all understand that healing is a process; it is not usually a quick fix. If you are currently sick in your body, you must be patient and allow God to perform healing in your body, from the crown of your head to the soles of your feet. His Word offers comfort in Isaiah 53:5 by letting us know that, "...He was wounded for our transgressions; he was bruised for our iniquities: the chastisement of our peace was upon him; and with his stripes we are healed."

Be Made Whole in Your Spirit

I am certain that many of us have experienced sickness in our bodies at some point in our lives, and we already received healing by the power of God. We followed the physician and the Physician's (God) instructions, and our healing manifested at the appointed time. I must share that some of us have also been spiritually sick. We need to be strengthened in our spirits.

Just like God healed our physical bodies, He can also heal us spiritually. Many of us so greatly need a spiritual touch from the Great Physician in this season of our lives. Are you ready to be healed spiritually? Are you ready to see spiritual healing take place in the body of Christ? I certainly am.

I explained in a previous chapter about the Woman's Eve Syndrome and how it has caused spiritual stagnation, hurt and pain, chaos, division in the church, among so many other things that is plaguing the entire body of Christ. This syndrome must be indentified by Christians as one that is operating deep within every aspect of humanity. Since we now know that Woman's Eve Syndrome is a man's fear of woman's influence and what it has done to the body of Christ, we must now turn to the Great Physician for spiritually healing.

We all have been exposed to a mutation which is a change in DNA (deoxyribonucleic acid), the hereditary material of life, and we need to be healed in our spirits. Notice the word *rib* right in the middle of the word deoxyribonucleic. Remember, Genesis 2:22 talks about the woman being made from the rib of Adam. Woman was inside Adam from the beginning. Notice the word *here* is the first four letters of the word hereditary. The Woman's Eve Syndrome is still here. We can see how fear has formed a bridge between men and women. Fear does not come from God. It is a foul spirit that has caused an epidemic within the body of Christ, and every relationship in Heaven and on Earth. It is still spreading through non-treatment. It is time to make an appointment with the Great Physician. It is time for our families to make an appointment…it is time for our government to make an appointment…it is time for our spiritual leaders to make an appointment…it is time for the body of Christ to make an appointment with the Great Physician.

We must understand that the first line of defense in the body is our skin. It is armour that covers us from head to toe. It is the largest body system. The first line of defense in the body of Christ is family; that's why Satan attacked it in the Garden of Eden, and now it has launched a full assault on family inside and outside of the body of Christ.

Let us use the data of the physician questionnaire in a spiritual sense. Our "Great Physician" has been on duty. He has indentified that there is a deviation of normal, spiritual body functioning, and it is causing a spiritual weakening within the body of Christ:

1. An increase in divorce rate in the church.
2. An increase in single-parent homes.
3. An increase in acceptance of gay marriages.
4. An increase in acceptance of gay couples adopting.
5. An increase in acceptance of transgender life style.
6. Increased assaults with and without weapons on church property.
7. An increase in the rate of infidelity.
8. An increase in acceptance of fornication
9. An increase in acceptance of sexist behavior.
10. An increase in domestic violence and domestic violence murders.

11. An increase in addictions, drugs, sex and alcohol.
12. A decrease in church attendance.
13. Continuous fighting over church doctrine and spiritual positions. These are just to name a few.

These are signs of objective disease:
1. An increase in sexual assaults against women and children.
2. An increase in bullying.
3. An increase in teen suicide.
4. An increase in the cases of hate crimes.

These are signs of subjective disease:
1. Racial tension.
2. Depression.
3. Body shaming.

I want you to understand that once Adam disobeyed God, our DNA suffered a mutation; our hereditary material of life was altered. This organism affected how we behave and its physiology. It changed every aspect of our lives. The organism becomes a host that would withstand barriers that could destroy it by the normal accounts of how the body fights against something that opposes its existence. This mutation eventually killed the first Adam. The Woman's Eve Syndrome curse is a primordial curse that is woven into molecular structure of humanity, and resulting in the parallel death of the physical and spiritual man.

God was well aware that the sacrifices of bullock and pigeons were just band aids. The cure was lying in His bosom. It was activated and manifested at God's appointed time. Now that there is no longer ignorance to this syndrome, the cure was lying in the bosom of God. The Great Physician has written a plan of care throughout the Holy Bible.

It is time to follow the Doctor's order by:

1. Repenting in the name of Jesus for allowing the curse to operate in all aspects of your life.
2. Asking those that you infected with the Woman's Eve Syndrome to forgive you.
3. Rebuking the spirit of fear (2 Timothy 1:7). That is what the Woman's Eve Syndrome is, the fear of woman's influence. Adam blamed his wife for his failure. Who have you blamed for your failures? Ask them to forgive you.
4. Accepting and recognizing that Jesus has restored God's perfect will. Just like in the Garden of Eden, men and women are joint heirs to the Kingdom of God through our King Jesus.
5. Having a peace treaty (between men and women) announced and honored by family and friends, churches, etc.

6. Teaching sound doctrine that women are called equal partners, not subordinates to any man but only Christ. You cannot possibly respect Christ and not His creation. There must be an integration of the Holy Spirit in every aspect of our lives. He will lead and guide us in all the ways of truth.
7. Respecting a woman's calling. It is no different than a man's calling in ministry, in business, in every aspect of life.
8. Training about the Woman's Eve Syndrome and how deadly it is when left untreated. This must be implemented.
9. Restructuring in leadership, family, business, etc. Jesus is the Head of everything, and man and woman are side by side.
10. Women and men speaking up against every form of sexism.
11. Standing and operating in your calling, knowing that God called you and not a person. There is nothing past or present that can stop God from using you for His Glory.

"We cannot solve our problems with the same thinking we used when we created them." –Albert Einstein

ELDER YOLANDA PATTERSON'S PICTURES

God kept me for a time such as now.

This photo was taken by Elder Robert Shack

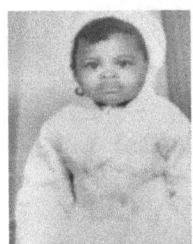

ELDER YOLANDA PATTERSON'S PICTURES

Notice the Angels in the upper right corner of my wedding picture.

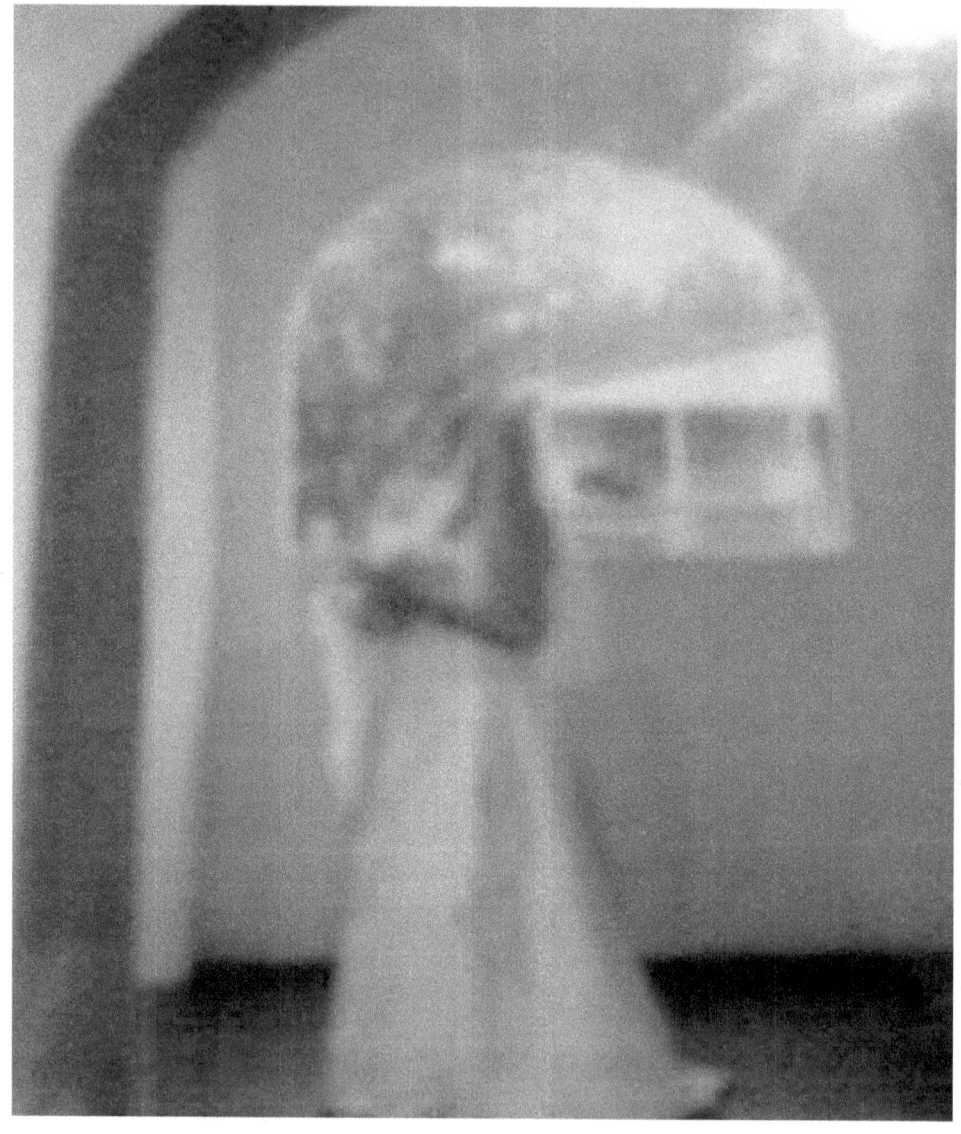

This photo was taken by Ms. Debi Tubbs

PRAYERS

PRAYER *FOR* REPENTANCE

Dear Heavenly Father, I pray that You steer the person who is reading this book to that place of repentance. Lord, sometimes we do things that appear to be right in our own eyes, but they are wrong and sinful in your sight. Lord, I ask that You help this person to see that they need to repent and turn from any wrongful doings or sin they may be committing now. Remind them of what You said in Acts 3:19, "Repent ye therefore, and be converted, that your sins may be blotted out, when the times of refreshing shall come from the presence of the Lord." I humbly ask that You hear my prayer and respond suddenly. I seal this prayer in the mighty name of Jesus. Amen.

Reader, I encourage you to read Acts 3:19, Acts 17:30, and Luke 5:32. Decree and declare that you will repent and turn from any sin that you may have committed.

PRAYER *FOR* FORGIVENESS

Dear Heavenly Father, I pray that You help the person who is reading this book to forgive anyone who they have not forgiven. Lord, I ask that You remove unforgiveness out of the space in their heart where the love of You should be flowing freely. Remind them of the warning You gave all of us in Matthew 6:15, "… if you do not forgive others their sins, your Father will not forgive your sins." I humbly ask that You hear my prayer and respond suddenly. I seal this prayer in the mighty name of Jesus. Amen.

Reader, I encourage you to read Matthew 6:14-15. Decree and declare that you will forgive anyone that you may not have forgiven so that you can be forgiven by Your Heavenly Father.

PRAYER *FOR* HEALING

Dear Heavenly Father, I pray that you heal the person who is reading this book mind, body, spirit, heart and soul. If they are sick in their body, I ask that You touch them right now. Lord, You said in Isaiah 53:5 that we are healed by Your stripes. Allow Your Word to come alive in this person's life. Reveal Yourself through Your Word so that they can know that You are with them and You will heal them from the crown of their head to the soles of their feet. I humbly ask that You hear this prayer and respond suddenly. I seal this prayer in the mighty name of Jesus. Amen.

Reader, I encourage you to read Isaiah 53:5. Decree and declare that you are healed by His stripes.

PRAYER *FOR* LOVE

Dear Heavenly Father, I pray that You help the person who is reading this book to love just as You commanded all of us to do in John 15:12. If they are bitter and lack love, allow them to repeatedly read this and other scriptures on love until it is deeply rooted in their heart and spirit, and they are able to love all mankind. I humbly ask that You hear my prayer and respond suddenly. I seal this prayer in the mighty name of Jesus. Amen.

Reader, I encourage you to read John 15:12. Decree and declare that you are able to love everyone with the Love of God.

PRAYER *FOR* RESTORATION

Dear Heavenly Father, I pray that You restore the person who is reading this book to a better state than they were before they lost their joy, peace…and even some material things. Lord, I know that the devil came to steal…but You assure us in Proverbs 6:31 that He MUST pay back seven times what he stole. And Lord, You even promised us in Joel 2:25 that You will restore to us the years that the locust hath eaten, the cankerworm, and the caterpiller, and the palmerworm, my great army which I sent among you." I humbly ask that You hear my prayer and respond suddenly. I seal this prayer in the mighty name of Jesus. Amen.

Reader, I encourage you to read Proverbs 6:31 and Joel 2:25. Decree and declare that everything that was stolen from you will be fully restored.

PRAYER *FOR* FAITH

Dear Heavenly Father, I pray that You increase the person who is reading this book level of faith so that they can receive more of what You have for them. Lord, sometimes situations and circumstances can make some of the best of us lose faith. I know that it is so very important that we all have faith, because it is impossible to please You without it. God, this person needs You to move for them right now. Help them to activate their faith. I humbly ask that You hear my prayer and respond suddenly. I seal this prayer in the mighty name of Jesus. Amen.

Reader, I encourage you to read Matthew 17:20 and Hebrews 11:6. Decree and declare that you will activate your faith and trust God unlimited.

PRAYER *FOR* HOPE

Dear Heavenly Father, I pray that You help the person who is reading this book remain hopeful and optimistic. Lord, help them to take their eyes off their situations, failures, and even the people who let them down! Speak to them right in the midst of their valley experience, Lord. Reassure them that Your plan is to give them hope and a future, just as You told prophet Jeremiah in the book of Jeremiah 29:11. I humbly ask that You hear my prayer and respond suddenly. I seal this prayer in the mighty name of Jesus. Amen.

Reader, I encourage you to read Jeremiah 29:11. Decree and decree and declare that you will prosper and keep your hope in Jesus Christ, and not man or woman.

PRAYER *FOR* SANITY

Dear Heavenly Father, I pray that You help the person who is reading this book keep their sanity. Lord, sometimes we encounter things that trouble our minds and make us do things out of character. Lord, I ask that You to renew their mindset and give them that same mind that was in Christ Jesus so they can focus clearly and think on those things above. (Philippians 2:5). And Lord, let them be "renewed in the attitude of their mind," just as You instructed in Ephesians 4:23. I humbly ask that You hear my prayer and respond suddenly. I seal this prayer in the mighty name of Jesus. Amen.

Reader, I encourage you to read Philippians 2:5, Ephesians 4:23 and Romans 12:12. Decree and declare that your mind will be renewed and your thoughts will be Holy and acceptable in the sight of God.

PRAYER *FOR* PEACE

Dear Heavenly Father, I pray that You give the person who is reading this book peace in the midst of their situation. Lord, please block the things the devil is throwing their way to strip them of their peace. Lord, I ask that You help them to pursue peace even more when their enemies rise up against them. And Lord, I ask that You whisper in their ear and let them know that "the peace of You…will guard their hearts and mind in Christ Jesus." (Philippians 4:7). I humbly ask that You hear my prayer and respond suddenly. I seal this prayer in the mighty name of Jesus. Amen.

> Reader, I encourage you to read Philippians 4:7, Psalm 85:8, and Isaiah 26:3. Decree and declare that you will keep your mind on Jesus and have perfect peace that only comes from Him.

PRAYER *FOR* WISDOM

Dear Heavenly Father, I pray that You grant the person who is reading this book wisdom. Lord, help them to understand the precious gift of having wisdom and give them a desire for wisdom. Let them know that using wisdom in all of their decisions is conducive to their spiritual growth. Remind them of what You said in Ecclesiastes 2:26, "To the person who pleases him, God gives wisdom, knowledge and happiness…" I humbly ask that You hear my prayer and respond suddenly. I seal this prayer in the mighty name of Jesus. Amen.

Reader, I encourage you to read Ecclesiastes 2:26, Psalm 37:30, James 1:5 and James 3:17. Decree and declare that the wisdom of God will be released to you in this season.

PRAYER *FOR* STRENGTH

Dear Heavenly Father, I pray that You strengthen the person who is reading this book. Lord, sometimes we get weak on our journey, and we feel like throwing in the towel. Lord, I ask that You lift this person up with Your right hand of mercy; keep them in the palm of Your hand and allow their strength to be made full in You. Teach them how to speak Your Word firmly when they are going through trials and tribulations in their life. Let them find comfort in Philippians 4:13, "I can do all things through Christ which strengthens me." I humbly ask that You hear my prayer and respond suddenly. I seal this prayer in the mighty name of Jesus. Amen.

Reader, I encourage you to read Philippians 4:13 and Nehemiah 8:10. Decree and declare that you will have more than enough strength to make it through any situation, and you will not give up on yourself or God.

PRAYER *FOR* COURAGE

Dear Heavenly Father, I pray that You give the person who is reading this book courage. Lord, don't let them fear anyone or anything. Lord, just as You told Joshua to, "Be strong and courageous. Do not be afraid; do not be discouraged, for the Lord your God will be with you wherever you go," assure this person that they can have confidence that You will be with them too, and they don't have to fear nor feel discouraged. I humbly ask that You hear my prayer and respond suddenly. I seal this prayer in the mighty name of Jesus. Amen.

Reader, I encourage you to read Joshua 1:9 and Deuteronomy 31:6. Decree and declare that you will not be overcome by fear, but you will be strong and courageous and go where God is leading you.

PRAYER *FOR* ANOINTING

Dear Heavenly Father, I pray that You anoint the person who is reading this book from head to toe. Lord, I ask that You lift every burden and destroy every yoke. Your Word says, "…and the yoke shall be destroyed because of the anointing." (Isaiah 10:27). Lord, I pray that You speak to them in this season and let them know that "no weapon formed against them shall prosper" and no weapon is strong enough to shatter Your anointing. I humbly ask that You hear my prayer and respond suddenly. I seal this prayer in the mighty name of Jesus. Amen.

Reader, I encourage you to read Isaiah 10:27, Decree and declare that God will anoint you afresh and that His anointing will destroy everything the devil may try to harm you with.

PRAYER *FOR* OBEDIENCE

Dear Heavenly Father, I pray that You teach the person who is reading this book how to be obedient. Lord, I ask that You help them to understand how important it is to You that we obey Your commandments, instructions and Word. Remind them of what You promised us in Isaiah 1:19, "If you are willing and obedient, you will eat the good of the land." Lord, I pray that You forgive them for being disobedient. I humbly ask that You hear my prayer and respond suddenly. I seal this prayer in the mighty name of Jesus. Amen.

Reader, I encourage you to read Isaiah 1:19. Decree and declare that you will obey the Lord for the rest of your life, so that you can always eat the good of the land.

PRAYER *FOR* GOD'S TIMING

Dear Heavenly Father, I pray that You allow the person who is reading this book to stay and flow in Your timing. Lord, don't let them get too impatient and step outside of Your divine timing, and Your perfect will. Your Word tells us in Isaiah 40:31 that "…they that wait upon the LORD shall renew their strength; they shall mount up with wings as eagles; they shall run, and not be weary; and they shall walk, and not faint." Lord, let them know that You will make sure they are in the right place at the right time as they continue flowing in Your divine timing. I humbly ask that You hear my prayer and respond suddenly. I seal this prayer in the mighty name of Jesus. Amen.

Reader, I encourage you to read Isaiah 40:31. Decree and declare that you will stay in God's divine timing.

PRAYER *FOR* HUMILITY

Dear Heavenly Father, I pray that You humble the person who is reading this book. Lord, You tell us in James 4:6 that You "...Oppose the proud but gives grace to the humble," and Your Word says in James 4:10 to, "Humble yourselves before the Lord, and he will lift you up." Lord, this person desires to walk in humility, and they need Your help along the way. I humbly ask that You hear my prayer and respond suddenly. I seal this prayer in the mighty name of Jesus. Amen.

Reader, I encourage you to read James 4:6 and James 4:10. Decree and declare that you will humble yourself before the Lord.

PRAYER *FOR* GUIDANCE

Dear Heavenly Father, I pray that You guide the person who is reading this book. Allow them to seek Your face in all things. Lord, they need Your advice even now on matters that require immediate attention. I ask that You provide the ultimate solution. Lord, please don't let them try to do it on their on and deviate from the path that You have ordained for them to take. Your Word confirms in Psalm 37:23 that, "The steps of a good man are ordered by the Lord: and he delighteth in his way." I humbly ask that You hear my prayer and respond suddenly. I seal this prayer in the mighty name of Jesus. Amen.

Reader, I encourage you to read Luke Psalm 37:23. Decree and declare that you will accept and follow God's leading in all matters of your life.

PRAYER *FOR* RESPECT

Dear Heavenly Father, I pray that You help the person who is reading this book to be respectful to others and be respected by others. Lord, sometimes we may not be aware of the subtle things we do that are disrespectful to someone. Lord, I ask that You help this person to be mindful of what they do and say to someone else. Let them know that everyone deserves to be respected at all times, including them. You tell us in 1 Peter 2:17 to, "Show proper respect to everyone, love the family of believers, fear God, honor the emperor." I humbly ask that You hear my prayer and respond suddenly. I seal this prayer in the mighty name of Jesus. Amen.

Reader, I encourage you to read 1 Peter 2:17 and Romans 12:10. Decree and declare that you will give respect to others and receive respect from others.

PRAYER *FOR* POWER

Dear Heavenly Father, I pray that You give the person who is reading this book the power to overcome. Lord, let them know that they are more than a conqueror in You. Your Word says in Luke 10:19, "I have given you authority to trample on snakes and scorpions and to overcome all the power of the enemy; nothing will harm you." Lord, let them know that you are with them as You already declared in 1 John 4:4, "…Greater is he that is in you, than he that is in the world." Let Your power rise up on the inside of them right now, Lord. I humbly ask that You hear my prayer and respond suddenly. I seal this prayer in the mighty name of Jesus. Amen.

Reader, I encourage you to read Luke 10:19 and 1 John 4:4. Decree and declare that you have the power to overcome anything.

PRAYER *FOR* MERCY

Dear Heavenly Father, I pray that You wrap your mercy around the person who is reading this book. Lord, I ask that You shield them from harm and danger. Lord, reassure them that "surely, goodness and mercy" shall follow them all the days of their life." (Psalm 23:6). I humbly ask that You hear my prayer and respond suddenly. I seal this prayer in the mighty name of Jesus. Amen.

Reader, I encourage you to read Psalm 23:6. Decree and declare that surely, goodness and mercy will always be with you.

PRAYER *FOR* GRACE

Dear Heavenly Father, I pray that You shower the person who is reading this book with Your grace. Lord, let them know that Your grace is "sufficient enough" for them. I ask that You remind them of the last time you allowed Your grace to walk them through the valley of the shadow of death. Lord, I thank You for being "full of grace and truth." I humbly ask that You hear my prayer and respond suddenly. I seal this prayer in the mighty name of Jesus. Amen.

Reader, I encourage you to read 2 Corinthians 12:9 and John 1:14. Decree and declare that the grace of God is sufficient enough for you.

PRAYER *FOR* DELIVERANCE

Dear Heavenly Father, I pray that You deliver the person who is reading this book from any strongholds, addictions, witchcraft, abuse, or anything else that may have them bound. Lord, I ask that You break every generational curse in their bloodline. Let them know that You have dominion over their life and no stronghold, addiction…can control them and hinder them from fulfilling their God-given purpose. Lord, I pray that You give Your Angels charge over them just as you declared in Psalm 91. I humbly ask that You hear my prayer and respond suddenly. I seal this prayer in the mighty name of Jesus. Amen.

Reader, I encourage you to read Psalm 91. Decree and declare that you will be delivered from anything that may have you bound in this season.

THE SERENITY PRAYER

God, give me grace to accept with serenity
the things that cannot be changed;
Courage to change the things
which should be changed;
and the wisdom to distinguish
the one from the other.

Living one day at a time,
Enjoying one moment at a time,
Accepting hardship as a pathway to peace,
Taking, as Jesus did,
This sinful world as it is,
Not as I would have it,
Trusting that You will make all things right,
If I surrender to Your will,
So that I may be reasonably happy in this life,
And supremely happy with You forever in the next.
Amen.

Reinhold Niebuhr

JOURNAL

Share your personal experiences and allow God to heal you as you release

JOURNAL

WOMAN'S EVE SYNDROME JOURNAL

JOURNAL

JOURNAL

JOURNAL

CONTACT INFORMATION

Elder Yolanda Patterson
P. O. Box 644
Lincoln, Al 35096
Email: minister81264@gmail.com
Website: www.yolandapatterson.com

www.ingramcontent.com/pod-product-compliance
Lightning Source LLC
Chambersburg PA
CBHW071411160426
42813CB00085B/1072